Searchlight BOOKS™

Do You
Know the
Continents?

Learning about Asia

Andrea Wang

Lerner Publications ◆ Minneapolis

Content Consultant: William Beeman, PhD, Professor of Anthropology, University of Minnesota

Lerner Publications Company
A division of Lerner Publishing Group, Inc.
241 First Avenue North
Minneapolis, MN 55401 USA

For reading levels and more information, look up this title at www.lernerbooks.com.

Library of Congress Cataloging-in-Publication Data

Wang, Andrea, author.
    Learning about Asia / by Andrea Wang.
        pages cm. — (Searchlight books. Do you know the continents?)
    Audience: Ages 8–11.
    Audience: Grades 4 to 6.
    Includes bibliographical references and index.
    ISBN 978-1-4677-8014-8 (lb : alk. paper) — ISBN 978-1-4677-8347-7
(pb : alk. paper) — ISBN 978-1-4677-8348-4 (eb pdf)
        1. Asia—Juvenile literature. I. Title.
    DS5.W36 2015
    950—dc23   2014044098

Manufactured in the United States of America
1 – VP – 7/15/15

Contents

Chapter 1
THE LARGEST
CONTINENT . . . page 4

Chapter 2
COUNTRIES AND
CITIES . . . page 8

Chapter 3
LANDFORMS AND CLIMATE . . . page 14

Chapter 4
NATURAL RESOURCES . . . page 20

Chapter 5
PEOPLE AND CULTURES . . . page 25

Chapter 6
ECONOMICS . . . page 32

Exploring Asia • 37
Glossary • 38
Learn More about Asia • 39
Index • 40

THE LARGEST CONTINENT

Asia is the world's largest continent. It is bigger than North America and South America combined! Approximately one-third of all the land on Earth is part of Asia. Europe and Africa border Asia to the west. Huge oceans lie to the north, east, and south of the continent.

Asia is huge! How much of the world's land is in Asia?

ASIA COVERS MORE THAN 17 MILLION SQUARE MILES (44 MILLION SQUARE KILOMETERS).

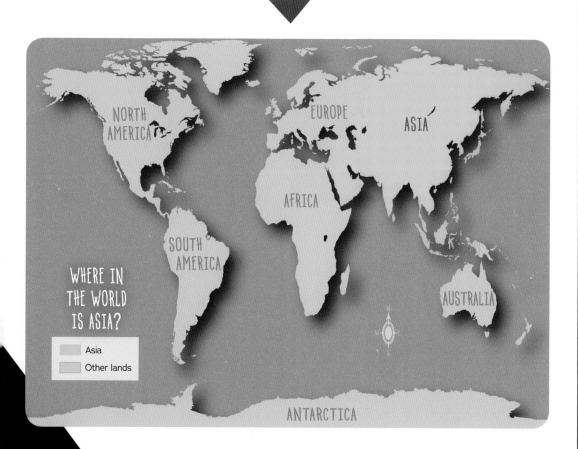

WHERE IN THE WORLD IS ASIA?

Asia

Other lands

NORTH AMERICA

EUROPE

ASIA

AFRICA

SOUTH AMERICA

AUSTRALIA

ANTARCTICA

The Dead Sea is approximately nine times saltier than the ocean.

Land of Extremes

Asia is wildly diverse in land, climate, and people. Asia's Himalaya Mountains are the highest in the world. Asia also has the lowest place on Earth, the Dead Sea. North Asia is freezing cold. South Asia is steamy and hot.

More than 4.3 billion people call Asia home. That's more than any other continent! They live in cities, villages, and rural areas. Asians speak many languages. They follow dozens of religions and lifestyles.

If you visit an Asian city, be ready for crowds.

Chapter 2

COUNTRIES AND CITIES

People have lived in Asia for more than one million years. Some of the earliest Asians lived in South Asia. Others lived in what is now northern China. People have spread all over Asia since then.

Asia has a long history. How long have people lived in Asia?

Drawing Boundaries

Asia has approximately forty-nine countries. Why is there no exact count? Taiwan considers itself a country. But China claims that Taiwan is part of China. Also, Russia and Turkey are part of both Europe and Asia. As a result, sometimes they are counted as Asian countries and sometimes they are considered nations of Europe. Without Taiwan, Russia, and Turkey, Asia would have only forty-six countries.

The Ural Mountains usually mark the border between Europe and Asia.

FIND TURKEY AND RUSSIA. DO YOU THINK THEY SHOULD BE IN EUROPE, ASIA, OR BOTH? WHERE WOULD YOU DRAW THE BORDER BETWEEN ASIA AND EUROPE?

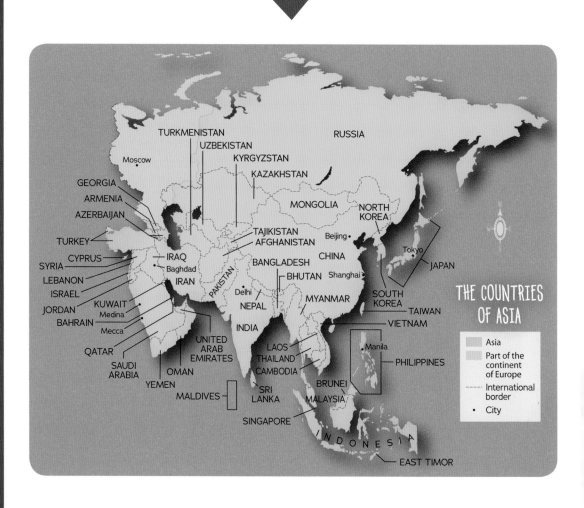

Moscow

TURKMENISTAN
UZBEKISTAN
KYRGYZSTAN
KAZAKHSTAN

RUSSIA

GEORGIA
ARMENIA
AZERBAIJAN

MONGOLIA

NORTH
KOREA

TURKEY

TAJIKISTAN
AFGHANISTAN

Beijing

CYPRUS
SYRIA
LEBANON
ISRAEL
JORDAN
BAHRAIN

IRAQ
Baghdad
IRAN

KUWAIT
Medina

Mecca

QATAR

SAUDI
ARABIA

YEMEN

PAKISTAN

OMAN

UNITED
ARAB
EMIRATES

BANGLADESH
BHUTAN

Delhi

NEPAL

INDIA

MALDIVES

SRI
LANKA

SINGAPORE

CHINA

Shanghai

MYANMAR

LAOS
THAILAND
CAMBODIA

Tokyo

JAPAN

SOUTH
KOREA
TAIWAN

VIETNAM

Manila

PHILIPPINES

BRUNEI
MALAYSIA

I N D O N E S I A

EAST TIMOR

THE COUNTRIES OF ASIA

Asia

Part of the continent of Europe

International border

• City

Diverse Countries

The biggest countries in Asia are Russia, China, and India. Russia is the largest country in area. More than 142 million people live in Russia. Eleven million of them live in the capital of Moscow. Not many people live in northern Russia, called Siberia. It is too cold! The coldest temperature on Earth outside of Antarctica was recorded in Siberia. It was –90°F (–68°C). And winter there is long. Much of Russia is covered in snow for more than half the year. It's no wonder Russians love winter sports such as skiing.

Would you like to live somewhere as cold as Siberia?

China is south of Russia. It is on Asia's eastern coast. China has more people than any other country. More than 140 Chinese cities have at least one million people. Only nine US cities are that big. Beijing is the capital of China. The city hosted the Olympics in 2008. Beijing has been an important city for centuries. It has been the center of China's government for most of the last two thousand years.

THE FORBIDDEN CITY IN BEIJING WAS HOME TO TWENTY-FOUR CHINESE EMPERORS.

India is southwest of China. The big peninsula reaches into the Indian Ocean. India is the second-most populous country after China. Delhi is India's capital. More than fifteen million people call the Delhi region home. Indians speak more than one thousand different languages. That's more than any other country.

Some island nations are part of Asia. Indonesia is made up of a huge chain of islands. It goes more than one-eighth of the way around the world!

Chapter 3

LANDFORMS AND CLIMATE

Three oceans surround most of Asia. The icy Arctic Ocean borders the continent to the north. The giant Pacific Ocean lies to the east. It meets up with the Indian Ocean in the south. The Indian Ocean borders Southeast Asia and the Middle East.

Three oceans surround Asia. Can you name them?

Several major lakes and rivers are in Asia. The Caspian Sea in western Asia borders five countries. It is the largest freshwater sea. Lake Baikal in Russia is smaller but deeper. Lake Baikal contains 20 percent of the world's freshwater. The Yangtze, Huang He, and Mekong Rivers flow through East and Southeast Asia. They are some of the longest rivers on the planet.

Hindus consider the Ganges River in India holy. They travel from far away to bathe in its waters.

The Harsh Gobi Desert

The Gobi Desert is in Mongolia and China. It is mostly dry soil and bare rock. Only 2 to 8 inches (5 to 20 centimeters) of rain fall there every year. The temperature drops to −40°F (−40°C) in January. Temperatures reach 113°F (45°C) in July. Plants, animals, and even people have adapted to the harsh conditions.

Look at Asia as seen from a satellite. What can you tell about Asia from the satellite image that you can't see on a map? Hint: Why are some areas brown, some green, and some white?

Mount Everest has always been special to local peoples. Local names for the mountain translate to "Goddess Mother of the World," "Goddess of the Valley," and "Ocean Mother."

Mountains and Islands

Asia has high mountains, vast plateaus, and many other special land features. The Himalayas run through several countries including India, Nepal, and Bhutan. You've probably heard of Mount Everest. The mountain is twenty-three times as tall as the Empire State Building!

Many islands and island chains dot the waters off Asia. These include Japan, the Philippines, and Borneo. More than seven thousand islands are part of the Philippines. But people live on only about one thousand of them.

Monsoons can cause big floods in Southeast Asia.

Hot and Cold

Asia has many different climates. Much of North Asia is tundra. Tundra areas have little rain or snow. They are very cold. More days are below freezing than above! Southern Asia has tropical and subtropical climates. These climates have high temperatures year-round. Tropical and subtropical areas have rainy and dry seasons. Each year in Asia brings monsoons. These strong winds and rains drench Asia in the rainy season.

FOLLOW THE COURSE OF THE YANGTZE RIVER. WHAT DIFFERENT CLIMATES DOES IT PASS THROUGH?

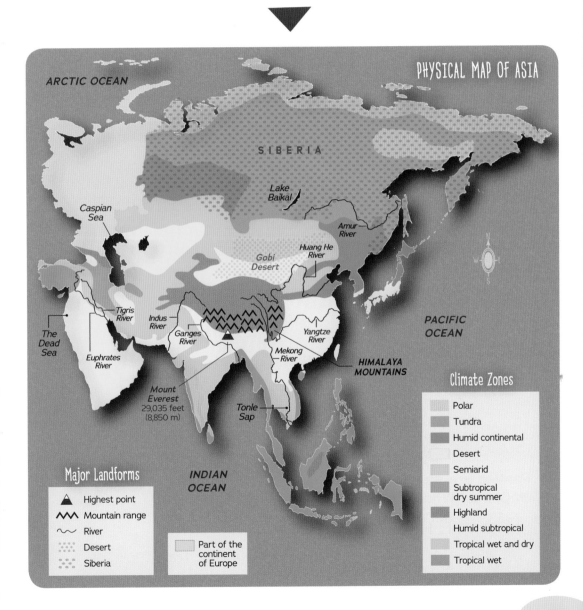

PHYSICAL MAP OF ASIA

ARCTIC OCEAN

SIBERIA

Lake Baikal

Caspian Sea

Amur River

Huang He River

Gobi Desert

Tigris River

Indus River

Ganges River

Yangtze River

PACIFIC OCEAN

The Dead Sea

Euphrates River

Mekong River

HIMALAYA MOUNTAINS

Mount Everest
29,035 feet
(8,850 m)

Tonle Sap

Climate Zones

Polar
Tundra
Humid continental
Desert
Semiarid
Subtropical dry summer
Highland
Humid subtropical
Tropical wet and dry
Tropical wet

Major Landforms

▲ Highest point
〜〜 Mountain range
〜 River
Desert
Siberia

INDIAN OCEAN

Part of the continent of Europe

Chapter 4

NATURAL RESOURCES

Asia is home to many rare animals. People come to see tigers and Komodo dragons. China is the only country with wild panda bears. Pandas like to munch on a giant grass called bamboo. It grows in Asia. Bamboo is used to make furniture, food, and paper.

Pandas are an important animal in China. What do pandas eat?

Snowy northern Asia is harsh. But animals still live there. Arctic foxes, hare, and reindeer survive cold temperatures thanks to their thick fur.

Southeast Asia's warm tropical climate is perfect for many animals. Apes and monkeys swing through the trees. Colorful birds, crocodiles, tigers, and rhinoceroses are just a few of the other animals that make their home in Asia.

Apes such as orangutans are well-suited to Southeast Asia's forests.

An oxen pulls a farm plow. What other types of animals might be useful for farming?

Beasts of Burden

Many of Asia's animals work for humans. Camels haul goods and supplies across deserts in the Middle East. In South Asia, elephants and oxen also carry goods. Some animals plow fields for farming.

Plant Life

Different areas of Asia are full of unique types of plants. Few plants can survive the cold temperatures in North Asia besides fir and pine trees. Central Asia is full of grasslands. Animals graze on the grasses. Valuable crops such as rubber, teak, nutmeg, and tea grow in wet Southeast Asia.

RICE IS GROWN IN FLAT SECTIONS CALLED TERRACES. TERRACED FIELDS MAKE IT EASIER TO DELIVER WATER TO CROPS.

Tonle Sap

Tonle Sap (BELOW) in Cambodia is the largest freshwater lake in Southeast Asia. Thousands of people make their homes right in the lake! Villagers build houses on wooden rafts or stilts. The houses rise and fall with the water. Most villagers are fishers. More than four hundred species of fish live in the lake. Other people plant rice and vegetables on land in the dry season.

Chapter 5

PEOPLE AND CULTURES

China and India have the most people in Asia. Maldives and Brunei are the smallest countries. Fewer than five hundred thousand people live in each.

China (BELOW) is home to many people. But not all Asian countries have giant populations. In which two Asian countries do the fewest people live?

Different Lands, Different Cultures

Just as populations vary across Asia, the continent's cultures are extremely diverse. The Arab culture is strong in the Middle East. The Middle East is a region of southwestern Asia. More than 75 percent of the people in the Middle East are Arab.

The Middle Eastern country of Israel (BELOW) is home to people of many different backgrounds, including both Arab and Jewish.

Saudi Arabia and Iraq are two countries with a large percentage of Arabs. Arabs speak Arabic. Many practice the religion Islam. Those who practice Islam are called Muslims. But not all Muslims live in the Middle East. More Muslims live in Indonesia than in any other country.

MUSLIMS WORSHIP IN
BUILDINGS CALLED MOSQUES.

▼

Russian culture spans northern Asia. Many Russians are Christians. Maslyanitsa is one folk holiday that Russians still celebrate. Maslyanitsa marks the end of winter. Russians eat traditional foods such as cabbage, potatoes, beets, and pancakes on this day.

Russian is an official language in Russia, Kazakhstan, and Kyrgyzstan. It uses its own alphabet called Cyrillic. You won't recognize the letters unless you speak Russian!

Russians eat traditional pancakes during the week of Maslyanitsa.

Indian culture fills South Asia. The official language of India is Hindi. But Indians speak many other languages as well. Most people practice Hinduism. In this religion, cows are considered sacred and are not eaten. There are also many Hindus in Nepal, Bhutan, and Bangladesh.

Holi is a spring festival celebrated by Hindus. People celebrate by throwing colored powder.

Ancient Civilizations

China has one of the oldest cultures. It has written records from approximately thirty-five hundred years ago. And the 5,500-mile (8,850 km) Great Wall of China took hundreds of years to build. Workers started building the wall in the 200s BCE. It still stands.

The Great Wall was built to protect China against invaders from the north.

A Holy Journey

The hajj is a religious journey. Muslims travel to Mecca in Saudi Arabia. Every adult Muslim is expected to make this journey at least once. The hajj takes place once a year. It lasts for five days. Muslims perform certain rituals on each day. Muslims have gone on the hajj for fourteen hundred years. Almost two million people perform the hajj each year.

Chapter 6

ECONOMICS

Asia produces a wide range of goods and resources. Many of them come from the earth. Most Asian nations use a lot of oil and coal for energy. Almost half the world's oil and coal comes from Asia.

Minerals are one of Asia's key resources. What kinds of mineral resources does Asia produce?

Asian mines supply iron, tungsten, and other rare minerals. Iron is used to make steel. Tungsten goes into electronic circuits and plane parts. There is probably tungsten from Asia in your computer!

Industry

More Asians work in mining, manufacturing, and construction than ever before. Many Middle Eastern countries produce oil and natural gas. Factories in Asia make clothing, shoes, electronics, and many other things that we use every day.

Rare metals mined in China are used in electronics such as phones and cameras.

ASIA HAS A WEALTH OF NATURAL RESOURCES. WHICH COUNTRIES PRODUCE THE WIDEST VARIETY OF RESOURCES?

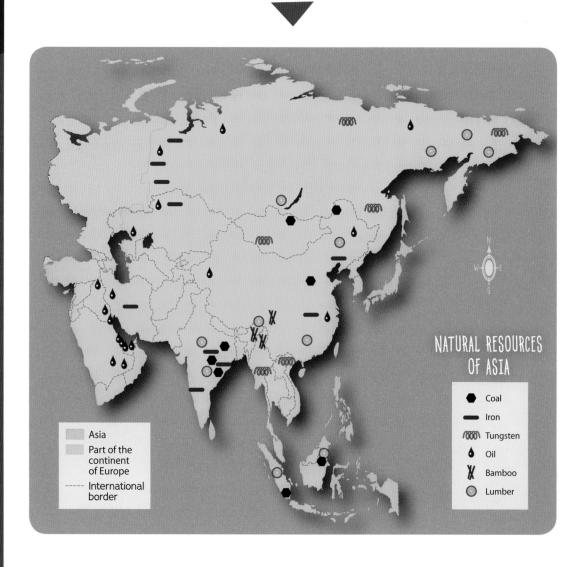

NATURAL RESOURCES OF ASIA

- ⬡ Coal
- ▬ Iron
- 〰 Tungsten
- 🌢 Oil
- ✗ Bamboo
- ◎ Lumber

Asia

Part of the continent of Europe

----- International border

The pollution in some Chinese cities is so bad that the air fills with smog and it is dangerous to breathe.

Asia's factories have helped its economy grow. But factories can cause problems. Some people in factories work in poor conditions. They make little money. Factories also produce pollution. Pollution can make people sick. It hurts the environment.

Service Jobs

Increased tourism in Asia has helped the number of service jobs grow. Service jobs include positions in restaurants, shops, hotels, banks, and other businesses that serve the public. People from all around the world visit Asia. Some come to see historical, religious, and cultural sites. Others visit to climb mountains. Or people relax on warm, sandy beaches.

Asian Adventure

Asia is a huge continent. It is full of more people and places than you could see in a lifetime. Its culture is ancient and amazing. Its animals are colorful and wild. Where will your adventure start?

Tourists visit Asia for unique adventures. What do you want to see first?

Exploring Asia

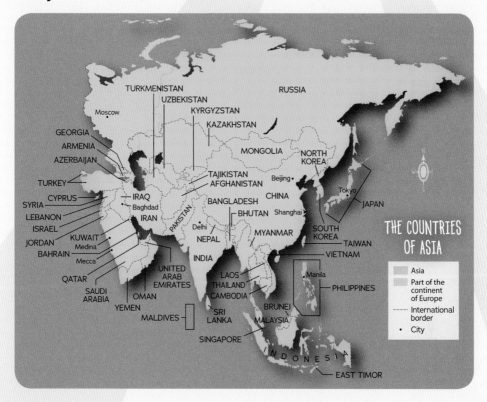

The map shows the following labels:

TURKMENISTAN
UZBEKISTAN
KYRGYZSTAN
KAZAKHSTAN
RUSSIA
Moscow
GEORGIA
ARMENIA
AZERBAIJAN
MONGOLIA
NORTH KOREA
TURKEY
CYPRUS
SYRIA
LEBANON
ISRAEL
JORDAN
BAHRAIN
QATAR
SAUDI ARABIA
YEMEN
MALDIVES
KUWAIT
Medina
Mecca
OMAN
IRAQ
Baghdad
IRAN
PAKISTAN
TAJIKISTAN
AFGHANISTAN
BANGLADESH
BHUTAN
Delhi
NEPAL
INDIA
UNITED ARAB EMIRATES
SRI LANKA
SINGAPORE
LAOS
THAILAND
CAMBODIA
Beijing
CHINA
Shanghai
MYANMAR
VIETNAM
SOUTH KOREA
TAIWAN
Tokyo
JAPAN
Manila
PHILIPPINES
BRUNEI
MALAYSIA
INDONESIA
EAST TIMOR

THE COUNTRIES OF ASIA

- Asia
- Part of the continent of Europe
- ----- International border
- • City

Choose two or three countries or cities from the map above that you want to know more about. Choose places from different parts of Asia. Research these places online. What sights can you see there? What do people eat? What local celebrations or festivals take place at the location? Write a paragraph about a trip that you will take to each place. What will you see and do?

Glossary

climate: a place's weather over a long period of time

continent: one of the seven divisions of land that make up Earth. Asia is the largest of the continents.

diverse: having many things that are different

freshwater: water that does not have salt. Most inland lakes are freshwater.

island: a piece of land surrounded by water. Asia has many of the world's largest islands.

monsoon: a period of long rains and wind. Monsoons come during Asia's rainy season.

peninsula: a piece of land surrounded by water on three sides. India is a peninsula.

region: a big geographic area. Asia has several regions, including the Middle East and Southeast Asia.

religion: the set of beliefs that a person holds. Asia's major religions include Buddhism and Hinduism.

ritual: something a person does as part of a ceremony

LERNER

SOURCE™

Expand learning beyond the printed book. Download free, complementary educational resources for this book from our website, www.lerneresource.com.

Learn More about Asia

Books

Athans, Sandra K. *Tales from the Top of the World: Climbing Mount Everest with Pete Athans.* Minneapolis: Millbrook Press, 2013. Experience what it's like to climb Mount Everest with Pete Athans, who has climbed to the top of the tallest mountain in the world seven times.

Drevitch, Gary. *Asia.* New York: Children's Press, 2009. This title presents surprising and interesting facts about people, places, and wildlife in Asia.

Ransom, Candice. *Tools and Treasures of Ancient China.* Minneapolis: Lerner Publications, 2014. Read about the ancient Chinese people, the tools they invented, and the treasures they made or discovered.

Websites

Asia: Enchanted Learning
http://www.enchantedlearning.com/geography/asia
Find a variety of resources for studying Asia, including map printouts, worksheets, and detailed information on different Asian countries.

Asia Society Kids
http://kids.asiasociety.org
Read stories, play games, and watch informative videos about Asia on this website. You can even learn some Hindi and Chinese words and phrases.

Kidipede
http://www.historyforkids.org
This website is full of information about ancient China, ancient India, the Turks and the Mongols, and the Islamic empire.

Index

Baikal, Lake, 15

Beijing, China, 12

Caspian Sea, 15

Dead Sea, 6

Delhi, India, 13

Gobi Desert, 16

Great Wall of China, 30

hajj, 31

Himalaya Mountains, 6, 17

Moscow, Russia, 11

Mount Everest, 17

Siberia, 11

Tonle Sap, 24

Yangtze River, 15

Photo Acknowledgments

The images in this book are used with the permission of: © Cao Jian Xiong/Thinkstock, p. 4;
© Laura Westlund/Independent Picture Service, pp. 5, 10, 19, 34, 37; © vvvita/iStock/Thinkstock,
p. 6; © saiko3p/Shutterstock Images, p. 7; © Rat007/Shutterstock Images, p. 8; © Nadezhda
Bolotina/Shutterstock Images, p. 9; © sfreestee/iStock/Thinkstock, p. 11; © 06photo/Shutterstock
Images, p. 12; © Pal Teravagimov/Shutterstock Images, p. 13; © Atikom/iStock/Thinkstock, p. 14;
© Radiokafka/Shutterstock Images, p. 15; © ASP GeoImaging/NASA/Alamy, p. 16; © Michal Zak/
iStock/Thinkstock, p. 17; © think4photop/Shutterstock Images, p. 18; © Leung Chopan/iStock/
Thinkstock, p. 20; © Anup Shah/Digital Vision/Thinkstock, p. 21; © soft light/Shutterstock Images,
p. 22; © Jimmy Tran/Shutterstock Images, p. 23; © takepicsforfun/iStock/Thinkstock, p. 24;
© TonyV3112/Shutterstock Images, p. 25; © JupiterImages/Photos.com/Thinkstock, p. 26;
© Vladimir Melnik/Shutterstock Images, p. 27; © Alexander Zemlianichenko/AP Images, p. 28;
© Adam Filipowicz/Shutterstock Images, p. 29; © Yuri Yavnik/AP Images, p. 30; © Zurijeta/
Shutterstock Images, p. 31; © abutyrin/Shutterstock Images, p. 32; © Bartlomiej Magierowski/
Shutterstock Images, p. 33; © hxdbzxy/iStock/Thinkstock, p. 35; © Natalia Deriabina/iStock/
Thinkstock, p. 36.

Cover image: © Planet Observer/Universal Images Group via Getty Images.

Main body text set in Adrianna Regular 14/20.
Typeface provided by Chank